Dear Anita and Cephas...
Happy Cooking!
Love,
Dave & Celeste
August 2009

Eat Your Way

with a wide variety of foods

to a Good Mood

NUTRITION AND THE PSYCHE

Everyone has an off day now and then when they might feel a bit depressed. All of our moods—the close interplay of emotions that occurs between our body and soul—are chemically controlled in the brain. The brain does this by using neurotransmitters such as serotonin and endorphins, which are generated as needed at the speed of light. Certain substances in the food we eat are involved in the generation of these neurotransmitters and can hence directly affect our productivity, behavior, and—last but not least—our moods.

PAY ATTENTION TO YOUR BRAIN'S SIGNALS

Good moods are closely linked with an overall feeling of relaxation, and with a rested body. If you are permanently stressed, you cannot expect to feel good in the long run. If you want to maintain a good mood, you should pay attention to the signals from your brain. Don't keep working when you're tired; instead, try to take a break. Energy drinks used as a quick pick-me-up really don't help in such cases—on the contrary, when they wear off, your stress and lack of motivation will be even greater than before.

MOOD ENHANCERS:

✳ Select foods containing substances that will optimize the processes in your brain and promote the generation of neurotransmitters.

✳ Make sure to get enough sleep—at least seven or eight hours a night for most people.

✳ Exercise! Exercise increases the serotonin levels in your brain and boosts the distribution of endorphins.

MOOD DETRACTORS:

✳ Main detractors to a good mood are saturated fatty acids. They need a great deal of oxygen to burn, which means that they impair (among other things) the transportation of oxygen to the brain. That makes you tired, listless, and even causes some people to become depressed. Animal products such as high-fat meats, bacon, sausage, high-fat cheeses, mayonnaise, many sweets, and high-fat pastries (such as cream pies) all contain high levels of saturated fatty acids.

✳ Increased alcohol consumption also has a negative effect on moods. On one hand, alcohol destroys B vitamins—the precise vitamins we desperately need to generate neurotransmitters. Small amounts of alcohol, however, can occasionally give a good mood a boost.

BRAIN FOOD

To ensure that our brain, which centrally controls all the body processes, can successfully meet its wide variety of tasks, it needs the following:

✳ Sufficient oxygen

✳ Sufficient energy in the form of glucose, the smallest unit of carbohydrates. Glucose should ideally be derived from whole grain breads, grains, potatoes, fresh vegetables, and fruit.

✳ Polyunsaturated fatty acids, which ensure that the protective coating of the nerve cells remains functional and that information is transmitted over the nerves as quickly as possible. Excellent sources of polyunsaturated acids are cold-pressed vegetable oils, nuts and seeds, and saltwater fish, such as mackerel, herring, tuna, and salmon.

✳ Amino acids, the smallest of the protein molecules, form the building blocks for neurotransmitters and hormones. Good sources include fish, shellfish, lean meat, eggs, milk and dairy products, cheese, grains, and legumes.

✳ A balanced intake of vitamins, minerals, and trace elements are essential for getting the biochemical processes going. These can be found in abundance in fresh vegetables and fruit, in grains and dairy products, lean meat, fish, nuts, seeds, and fresh herbs.

Mood-Enhancing

how to feel better every day

Brain Chemicals

BIOLOGICAL SUBSTANCES THAT MAKE YOU FEEL HAPPY

The neurotransmitters that transport information from one nerve cell to another are either substances that are supplied directly by our bodies or substances that are gained from our diet. Some neurotransmitters must first be generated in the brain. The building blocks for these types of neurotransmitters are usually amino acids, though additional vitamins, minerals, trace elements, or even fatty acids are frequently needed as well. Of the over 60 neurotransmitters discovered thus far, the following help to keep your mood on track:

SEROTONIN

This substance is also referred to as the "good mood hormone" because it plays the lead chemical role in feeling happy. If a sufficient amount is present, we feel balanced and happy. Serotonin promotes relaxation and a feeling of well-being and supports deep sleep. If the brain has an insufficient amount of serotonin, your mood rapidly deteriorates, and a lack of serotonin can even make you aggressive. This neurotransmitter is already contained in some foods, or it can be formed from tryptophan, an amino acid. More serotonin is formed when we consume less fat and more carbohydrates.

ACETYLCHOLINE

This neurotransmitter is synthesized from choline, which is a B vitamin. Among other things, acetylcholine promotes concentration, alertness, learning, and memory. This neurotransmitter keeps us mentally fit, optimistic, and relaxed. Some medications and drugs, however, can significantly disrupt the synthesis and effect of acetylcholine.

DOPAMINE

This neurotransmitter stimulates the heart, circulation, and metabolism. It can mobilize the body's energy sources. As a result, you are active and feel good. Dopamine affects our thoughts, and high concentrations can lead to exaggerated fantasies and brief lapses into daydreams. A huge deficit of dopamine can lead to a lack of motivation and even to emotional voids.

NOREPINEPHERINE

Aside from serotonin, norepinepherine is one of the most important happiness hormones. It has a stimulating effect on the brain, and it promotes perception, motivation, and energy. This neurotransmitter also acts as an antidepressant. New studies show that norepinepherine not only helps you focus in stressful situations, it may even make you feel optimistic and euphoric, which makes stress fun and invigorating. You can also thank norepinepherine for making memories of happy occasions or strong feelings particularly intense. The building block of norepinepherine is the amino acid phenylalanine.

ENDORPHINS AND NEUROPEPTIDES

Endorphins are a group of brain chemicals that act like drugs or natural narcotics. They can ease pain and trigger a sense of well-being as well as happy or euphoric feelings. When the endorphin level rises, it provides for a balanced psyche. Serotonin activates endorphins, while norepinepherine prevents the premature drop of these highly sensitive chemicals. Neuropeptides cause stimulating effects; among other things, they control our emotions as well as sexual behavior and eating patterns.

Foods to Improve
stimulating and invigorating foodstuffs
Your Mood

EATING WELL AND LAUGHING
GO HAND IN HAND

Among the various agents in food, there are a handful of substances that can intensify the positive effect of neurotransmitters, which include the following:

✳ Phytochemicals: Phytochemicals are a group of about 30,000 different bioactive, plant-derived substances, such as color, fragrance, and aroma components in foods, especially in fresh fruits and vegetables. They play a substantial role in maintaining a healthy and vital body.

✳ Spices: All spices soothe the soul. Saffron can help to increase a positive sense of well-being, while nutmeg and cinnamon help to brighten moods. The sweet flavor of vanilla releases endorphins, which also promote a sense of well-being.

✳ Capsaicin: This substance is responsible for the spiciness in paprika and chiles. Capsaicin also releases endorphins.

✳ Sinigrin: This substance found in mustard can boost alertness and activity, and hence support your zest for life.

✳ Stimulating agents: These substances are generated through components of oat

protein and result in the release of dopamine, which is in turn a precursor to serotonin. These stimulating agents not only promote concentration and productivity, but both oats and oatmeal brighten your moods.

✳ Caffeine: In studies, test subjects indicated that coffee (2 cups a day) gave them a clearer head, more self-confidence, and more energy. Caffeine probably enhances the effect of dopamine and norepinepherine, hormones that promote productivity. An excess of coffee, however, results in the exact opposite effect, making you nervous and jittery.

✳ Cocoa: Cocoa powder in chocolate contains quite a few highly effective substances that ease frustration and lovesickness and heighten the senses. Theobromine, for instance, stimulates the central nervous system, and phenylethylamine raises the serotonin level and has an invigorating effect.

NEURO-TRANSMITTER	HELPS WITH	GOOD SOURCES
Serotonin	Mood swings; cravings for sweets; restlessness; irritability; minor anxiety; sleep disturbances	Pasta, rice, potatoes, whole grains, whole grain bread, nuts, dates, figs, bananas, pineapple, sweets, legumes, tofu, red vegetables, radishes, fennel, dairy products, cheese, saltwater fish, shellfish, lean meats, poultry
Acetylcholine	Impaired concentration and learning; memory strain	Liver, egg yolks, cheese, oatmeal, soy, lecithin, legumes, whole grains, whole-grain breads, nuts, wheat germ, sesame seeds, brewers yeast
Dopamine	Impaired concentration; lack of motivation	Milk and dairy products, cheese, eggs, potatoes, rice, pasta, poultry, meat, fish, shellfish
Norepinepherine	Mental stress; sleep disturbances; depression; lack of concentration; lack of motivation	Milk and dairy products, fish, shellfish, eggs, poultry, meat, whole grains, legumes, red vegetables, spinach, apples, pineapple, nuts, chocolate
Endorphins and Neuropeptides	Stress; pressure to achieve; mood swings; listlessness and depression	Fish, meat, poultry, dairy products, whole grains, pasta, whole-grain breads, honey, bananas, dried fruit, chocolate and other sweets

Power

enhancing happiness through the food you eat

Week

BEATING THE BLUES

What can you do for yourself if you feel sad, tired, and unmotivated? For seven days, enjoy the following recipes. These recipes are both healthy and easy to prepare, and will enhance a good mood. All in all, this week will harmonize your mind, release positive energy, and make you feel happy.

7-DAY PLAN

In our 7-day plan, you will find suggestions for breakfast, lunch, and dinner for every day of the week. Feel free to mix and match meals any way you like, because all the recipes in this book contain the substances we have discussed that promote more balance and vitality. For those of you who are too busy to cook two meals a day, simply select a meal to prepare for dinner. You can always take along the two sandwiches from the breakfast chapter (page 16) for your lunches. Another ideal solution is whole-grain bread with a low-fat cheese, or Mozzarella Papaya Salad on page 27. Any fresh fruit, such as apples, pears, berries, bananas, figs, or pineapple, combined with yogurt or cottage cheese and a few nuts, always makes a good choice that can be enjoyed at work.

NATURAL ACTIVE AGENTS

The following list outlines how you can tailor foods to suit your own special needs:

* Protein-rich foods, such as milk and dairy products, fish, shellfish, and lean meat all support productivity and concentration, as do nuts, legumes, and wheat germ.

* The following herbs and spices contain stimulating agents: saffron, nutmeg, ginger, pepper, cinnamon, vanilla, peppermint, basil, and parsley.

* If relaxation is what you seek, turn to vegetables from the nightshade family, such as potatoes, tomatoes, and bell peppers, or you can indulge in grains, pasta, rice, and green vegetables.

* To support strong nerves, think about including the following in your diet: wheat germ, oatmeal, millet, rice, whole-grain bread, almonds, liver, and lean cuts of pork.

* To help reduce stress, turn to milk and dairy products, eggs, cheese, fish, lean meat, whole-grain products, potatoes, vegetables, fruit, nuts, and sesame seeds.

Eating Plan for the Week

Monday

* Muesli with Yogurt and Strawberries
* Tangy Tomato-Basil Shake ✳ Zucchini Pancakes with Cured Salmon
* Waldorf Salad with Pineapple

Tuesday

* Turkey Breast Sandwich
* Halibut with a Rice and Vegetable Crust
* Tex-Mex Wrap with Avocado ✳ Apricot-Cream Cheese Gratin

Wednesday

* Walnut-Berry Yogurt
* Mango Lassi with Maple Syrup ✳ Vegetable Curry with Peanuts
* Corn Fritters with Shrimp

Thursday

* Scrambled Eggs with Cheddar, served with whole-grain bread
* Stuffed Potatoes, served with a mixed greens salad
* Creamy Saffron Soup ✳ Pineapple-Papaya Salad

Friday

* Yogurt with Aloe Vera and Grapes
* Baked Tuna with Fennel, served with brown rice
* Couscous Salad with Red Vegetables

Saturday

* Gorgonzola Sandwich
* Vegetable Stew with Millet ✳ Chocolate Mousse
* Beet and Orange Salad, served with multigrain bread

Sunday

* Salmon Mousse, served with a whole-grain toast
* Spicy Chicken with Fresh Mango Sauce ✳ Creamy Citrus Cooler
* Red Lentil and Arugula Salad

Walnut-

with toasted oats

Berry

Yogurt

Serves 2: 1/4 cup rolled oats • 2 tbs walnuts • 12 oz low-fat plain yogurt
• 1–2 tsp floral honey • 4 oz mixed berries

Toast the oats in a small, dry nonstick skillet until golden brown, stirring constantly. Finely chop the walnuts, then add the nuts and the oatmeal to the yogurt, and sweeten to taste with honey. Spoon the yogurt into tall glasses and top off with the rinsed berries.

PER SERVING: 250 calories • 9 g protein • 13 g fat • 24 g carbohydrates

Muesli with Yogurt
naturally sweetened with maple syrup
and Strawberries

Serves 2: 1 banana • 4 oz fresh strawberries • 1/4 cup unsweetened muesli • 2 tbs wheat germ • 1 cup plain yogurt • 2 tsp maple syrup • 1 sprig fresh mint

Peel and slice the banana. Wash, trim, and quarter the strawberries. Arrange the fruit on one half of each plate. Mix the muesli and wheat germ together, then arrange next to the fruit. Pour the yogurt between the fruit and muesli, then drizzle with maple syrup. Garnish the muesli with mint.

PER SERVING: 190 calories • 7 g protein • 3 g fat • 42 g carbohydrates

Yogurt with Aloe Vera
a great source of vitamin C
and Grapes

Serves 2: 8 oz purple grapes • 2 cups plain yogurt • 1/4 cup aloe vera juice • 1 tsp vanilla extract • 2 tbs ground hazelnuts • Sugar or honey to taste • 1 tbs fresh lemon juice

Wash the grapes, remove stems, then cut in half lengthwise, and remove seeds if desired. Set aside. In a bowl, add yogurt and stir the aloe vera juice, vanilla extract, and ground hazelnuts into the yogurt, and add sugar or honey and lemon juice to taste. Fill two small glass bowls, alternating layers of grapes (use two thirds) and the yogurt mixture. Top off with the remaining one third of the grapes.

PER SERVING: 277 calories • 10 g protein • 11 g fat • 37 g carbohydrates

Scrambled Eggs
on hearty whole-grain bread
with Cheddar

Beat the eggs with the milk, salt, and pepper, until the egg mixture is smooth but not foamy. Melt the butter in a nonstick skillet over medium heat.

Add the egg mixture to the pan and cook slowly over low heat. Once it starts thickening, use a spatula to carefully draw the egg mixture from the outer edge into the center.

Wash and trim the bell pepper half, then chop it finely. Sprinkle the cheddar cheese and grated bell pepper over the scrambled eggs and wait for the cheese to melt. The eggs are finished once the mixture has completely thickened, but is still creamy and shiny. Arrange the scrambled eggs on the whole-grain bread slices and serve warm.

Serves 2:

3 eggs

1/4 cup milk

Salt to taste

White pepper to taste

1 tbs butter

1/2 small red bell pepper

1/4 cup grated cheddar cheese

4 slices whole-grain bread, toasted

Eggs

Eggs are among the most nutritious foods. In addition, they are an unusually rich source of fat-soluble vitamins as well as vitamins B2, B12, and folic acid. Lecithin, also contained in eggs, is an important nutrient for the brain and nerves. Tryptophan, an amino acid, is largely responsible for generating serotonin, a chemical that makes you feel good.

PER SERVING:

380 calories

20 g protein

21 g fat

27 g carbohydrates

Salmon
for Sundays and special occasions
Mousse

Serves 2:

3 oz smoked salmon
1 tbs olive oil
1 tbs soft butter
2 tbs sour cream
Salt to taste
Pepper to taste
1–2 tbs fresh lemon juice
1/2 bunch fresh chives
5 oz salmon fillet, cooked
4 slices whole-grain bread, toasted

Cut the smoked salmon into large pieces. Then, using a food processor or blender, finely puree the smoked salmon along with the olive oil, butter, sour cream, salt, pepper, and 1 tbs of the lemon juice. Wash the chives and shake dry, then use kitchen scissors to cut them finely. Cut the salmon fillet into small cubes, then add to the mousse along with the chives. Season to taste with salt, pepper, and the remaining lemon juice.

Refrigerate the salmon mousse until it is ready to serve. Serve the mousse with the crispy, warm whole-grain toast.

Omega-3 fatty acids for the brain

Of all fish, salmon is one of the richest sources of omega-3 fatty acids, which are vital for protecting nerve cells and accelerating their information flow. The amino acids and vitamins in salmon are involved in the generation of many substances that prevent depression and can enhance sensory perceptions. In other words, eating salmon is a pleasure that pays off by both making you feel good and be more motivated.

PER SERVING:

375 calories

32 g protein

19 g fat

18 g carbohydrates

Turkey Breast
a low-fat meal to go
Sandwich

Serves 2: 2 whole-grain rolls • 2 oz English hothouse cucumber • 1/2 red bell pepper • 2 oz cream cheese, softened • Black pepper to taste • 4 leaves romaine lettuce • 2 oz turkey breast, sliced

Split the rolls in half lengthwise. Wash and slice the cucumber. Wash the bell pepper half, trim, and dice finely. Mix the bell pepper into the cream cheese and season to taste with black pepper, then spread on one half of the rolls. Arrange the romaine, cucumber slices, and turkey breast on bottom half of the rolls, then top with the upper half of the rolls.

PER SERVING: 254 calories • 12 g protein • 14 g fat • 23 g carbohydrates

Gorgonzola
with fresh figs and pistachios
Sandwich

Serves 2: 1 tbs shelled pistachios • 2 long whole-grain rolls • 2 fresh, ripe figs • 4 oz Gorgonzola cheese • 4 leaves red leaf lettuce

Coarsely chop the pistachios and briefly toast in a dry nonstick skillet, then set aside to cool. Slice the rolls in half lengthwise. Wash the figs and pat dry. Cut the figs and Gorgonzola cheese into slices. Arrange the lettuce leaves, cheese, and figs on the bottom half of the rolls, sprinkle with the pistachios, then top with the upper halves of the rolls.

PER SERVING: 400 calories • 16 g protein • 19 g fat • 42 g carbohydrates

Ham Salad Sandwich
rich in bioactive agents
with Vegetables

Briefly drain the pickled vegetables in a sieve, then chop as finely as possible. Wash the apple, pat dry, then cut into quarters and remove the core. Chop the apple quarters into fine dice. Trim the fat from the ham, if necessary, then cut the ham into fine dice.

Stir the pickled vegetables, diced apple, and diced ham together in a bowl. Mix in the yogurt and mustard, then season to taste with the pepper. Spread the ham salad mixture onto the bread slices, cut the slices in half diagonally, then garnish with the minced chives and serve.

Serves 2:
About 2 oz mixed pickled vegetables
1 small apple
4 oz cooked ham
2 tbs plain yogurt
Mustard to taste
White pepper to taste
4 slices dark whole-grain bread (such as rye bread)
1 tbs minced fresh chives

The benefits of sour food

Pickled vegetables contain lactic acid bacteria, which have a beneficial effect on our metabolism. These bacteria protect us from harmful bacteria and fungi, thereby preventing infections and strengthening our immune system. This keeps the body healthy and fit.

PER SERVING:

370 calories

20 g protein

11 g fat

47 g carbohydrates

Beet and
rich in serotonin and phytochemicals
Orange Salad

Wash, peel, and dice the beets. Fill a pot with 1/3 cup water and the maple syrup, cover, and simmer the beets for 8-10 minutes over low heat.

Remove the beets from the heat and stir in the lemon juice and the sherry. Cover and refrigerate the beets overnight.

Drain the beets before serving. Peel the oranges, then cut in half, and cut into thin slices. Collect the juice in a bowl and add up to 2 tbs to the beets. Wash and trim the fennel bulb, then cut into paper-thin slices.

Stir together the remaining orange juice with some salt, pepper, and the oil, then drizzle over the fennel slices. Arrange the fennel and orange slices together with the beets on a plate. Coarsely chop the cashews and sprinkle over the salad before serving.

Serves 2:

8 oz small red beets

1 tbs maple syrup

2 tbs fresh lemon juice

2 tbs cream sherry

2 small oranges

1 small bulb fennel (about 5 oz)

Salt to taste

White pepper to taste

1 tbs olive oil

2 tbs cashews

PER SERVING: 250 calories • 6 g protein • 11 g fat • 28 g carbohydrates

Waldorf Salad
a refreshing source of vitamins
with Pineapple

Serves 2:
3 tbs shelled walnuts
4 oz celery
4 oz celery root (celeriac)
2 tbs fresh lemon juice
2 red apples
2 tbs milk
2 tbs reduced-fat mayonnaise
White pepper to taste
4 oz fresh pineapple

Coarsely chop 2 tbs of the walnuts. Wash and trim the celery, then cut the stalks into a fine dice and mince any of the greens. Peel the celery root, then wash and either grate the bulb or cut it into very fine dice. Immediately mix the celery root with the lemon juice.

Wash and dry the apples, then cut into quarters and remove the core. Cut the apples into fine dice. Add the diced apples to the grated or diced celery root.

Add the milk to the mayonnaise and stir until smooth, then season to taste with pepper. Stir in the celery root-apple mixture, the walnuts, the diced celery, and the celery greens. Cover and refrigerate the salad for one hour. Cut the pineapple into pieces and fold into the salad. Garnish with the remaining nuts and serve.

Walnuts

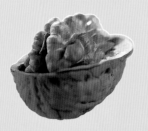

These aromatic nuts are packed with vital nutrients: amino acids, vitamins, minerals, as well as an abundance of unsaturated fatty acids. This powerful combination revitalizes your brain cells, combats fatigue and stress, promotes activity, and keeps you fit. Walnuts enhance your moods and your sense of well-being.

PER SERVING:

237 calories

5 g protein

12 g fat

33 g carbohydrates

Couscous Salad with

particularly rich in serotonin

Red Vegetables

Peel the carrot, onion, and garlic, then cut all into fine dice. Heat the oil in a saucepan over medium-low heat, then add the carrot, onion, and garlic and sauté lightly. Add the vegetable stock, cover, and simmer over low heat for 2 minutes. Stir in the couscous, bring to a boil, then remove the pot from the burner, cover, and let stand for the period of time specified on the package. Drain the couscous if necessary and cool. Wash and trim the tomatoes and bell pepper, then cut into small cubes. Wash the lettuce, shake dry, then tear into small pieces.

Stir together the vinegar, salt, pepper, and olive oil and stir in the vegetables and the lettuce. Season the couscous to taste with the lemon juice, salt, and pepper, then arrange on plates with the vegetables, lettuce, and fresh basil.

Serves 2:

1 carrot

1 small red onion

1 clove garlic

2 tsp vegetable oil

2/3 cup vegetable stock

1 cup couscous

2 small ripe tomatoes

1 small red bell pepper

4 leaves red leaf lettuce

3 tbs white wine vinegar

Salt to taste

Black pepper to taste

1 tbs extra-virgin olive oil

3-4 tbs fresh lemon juice

Fresh basil

Red vegetables

The colors of food as much as their actual nutrients influence the mind. Red symbolizes warmth, strength, and vitality. Vegetables such as tomatoes, red bell peppers, red beets, carrots, red beans, and red cabbage put new life into you, promote optimism and a positive outlook on life.

PER SERVING:

500 calories

13 g protein

14 g fat

79 g carbohydrates

Red Lentil and
with warm goat cheese
Arugula Salad

Heat the olive oil in a saucepan over medium heat and briefly sauté the rosemary. Add the lentils and vegetable stock, cover, and simmer for 10 minutes over low heat. Preheat the oven to 350°F.

Wash and trim the green onions, then cut into thin rings. Trim and sort the arugula leaves, then wash and shake dry before tearing into small pieces. Drain the lentils in a sieve. Stir together the vinegar, salt, pepper, and sunflower oil, then add 2 tbs of the mixture to the warm lentils. Peel and mince the garlic and add it to the lentils. Season the salad with salt and pepper. Score the goat cheese on both sides in the shape of a star. Place the goat cheese in a small oiled baking dish and bake until slightly melted, about 5-10 minutes. Fold the green onions, arugula, and remaining marinade into the lentil salad, then arrange on plates with the warm cheese.

Serves 2:

2 tsp olive oil

2 tsp chopped fresh rosemary leaves

4 oz red lentils

1 cup vegetable stock

2 green onions

1 bunch of arugula (about 2 oz)

2 tbs white wine vinegar

Salt to taste

White pepper to taste

1 tbs sunflower oil

1 clove garlic

2 small rounds of goat cheese (about 2 oz each)

Lentils

Like peas and beans, red lentils are a member of the legume family, are a great source of minerals, and are rich in vitamin B1, which is essential for keeping the brain and muscles fit. Red lentils also have a high content of vegetable protein and are a rich source of tryptophan, the building block of serotonin.

PER SERVING:

395 calories

23 g protein

20 g fat

31 g carbohydrates

Creamy Saffron
with leeks and toasted almonds
Soup

Toast the bread and cut it into small cubes. Peel the shallot and garlic, then chop both finely. Thoroughly wash and trim the leek before cutting into rings. Heat the oil in a saucepan over

Serves 2:
1 slice whole-grain bread
1 shallot
1 small clove garlic
1 small leek
1 tbs olive oil
1/2 tsp ground saffron
2 1/2 cups vegetable stock
3 tbs heavy cream
Salt to taste
White pepper to taste
1 tbs sliced almonds

medium heat, then add the leek, garlic, and shallot and sauté for 4 minutes. Remove a generous 1 tbs of the vegetable mixture from the pot and set aside.

Stir the bread cubes and saffron into the saucepan. Add the vegetable stock, bring to a boil, then cover and simmer gently for 30 minutes. Vigorously stir the heavy cream into the soup, then season to taste with salt and pepper.

Toast the sliced almonds in a small, dry, nonstick skillet until golden brown. Ladle the soup into warm bowls. Stir in the reserved vegetables and the toasted almond slices, then serve.

Saffron

Saffron is the most expensive spice in the world. It's made from the stigmas of a Mediterranean crocus, which are hand-picked and dried. Saffron gives dishes a distinctive yellow color and a slightly bittersweet flavor, while its bioactive substances and ethereal oils soothe the soul. Saffron's qualities as an aphrodisiac have been known since ancient times.

PER SERVING:

205 calories

4 g protein

13 g fat

16 g carbohydrates

Yogurt Soup with
tastes great with sesame flatbread
Red Pepper

Cut the bell pepper into quarters, remove the stem, seeds, and ribs, and wash. Cut the quarters crosswise into short, thin strips. Wash and trim the green onions, then cut them diagonally into thin slices. Peel and mince the garlic.

In a nonaluminum saucepan, whisk together the yogurt, meat stock, and egg. While whisking constantly, quickly bring the mixture to a boil over medium heat. Remove the pot from the heat and season with salt and pepper. Stir well occasionally.

Heat the olive oil in a small skillet, then sauté half each of the bell pepper, green onions, and garlic for 3 minutes while stirring constantly. Wash the mint, shake dry, and set aside several leaves for garnish.

Chop the remaining mint leaves. Using a hand blender or regular blender, quickly puree the soup, then ladle into warm serving bowls. Mix together the remaining vegetables and the chopped mint and sprinkle over the yogurt soup. Garnish with the reserved mint leaves and serve.

Serves 2:
1 red bell pepper
2 green onions
1 clove garlic
8 oz plain whole-milk yogurt
1 cup meat stock (homemade is best)
1 egg
Salt to taste
White pepper to taste
1 tbs olive oil
3 sprigs fresh mint

PER SERVING: 180 calories • 9 g protein • 12 g fat • 9 g carbohydrates.

Mozzarella and
with fresh basil and chile oil
Papaya Salad

Slit open the chile, then trim, wash, and cut it into paper-thin strips. Stir the chile with the oil and salt in a bowl and let stand for about 20 minutes.

Cut the mozzarella in half, then cut into very thin slices. Peel the papaya, cut in half lengthwise, and use a spoon to remove the seeds. Cut the papaya halves crosswise into slices. Wash the basil and shake dry, then remove the leaves from the stems. Decoratively arrange the mozzarella slices, papaya, and basil leaves on two plates and drizzle with the chile oil. Serve with the sunflower bread.

Serves 2:
1 small red chile
3 tbs soybean or canola oil
Pinch of salt
4 oz fresh mozzarella cheese
1 ripe papaya
3 sprigs fresh basil
Sunflower bread for accompaniment

Papaya—exotic power fruit

Papaya contains beta carotene, a substance that protects nerve cells from aggressive oxygen connections. Papain, an enzyme contained in papaya, gets the metabolism going, enhances fitness, and promotes a good mood.

PER SERVING:

450 calories

23 g protein

39 g fat

4 g carbohydrates

Mango Lassi with
a taste of India—rich in vitamins
Maple Syrup

Serves 2: 10 oz low-fat plain yogurt • 6 tbs mineral water • 1/4 cup mango nectar • 3 tbs fresh lemon juice • Maple syrup to taste • Fresh mint leaves

Using a whisk or blender, vigorously whip the yogurt with the mineral water, mango juice concentrate, and lemon juice until foamy. Sweeten the drink to taste with the maple syrup and pour into two tall glasses. Garnish with mint leaves.

PER SERVING: 165 calories • 5 g protein • 3 g fat • 30 g carbohydrates

Fruit Smoothie with
try fresh ginger as a tasty alternative
Wheat Germ

Serves 2: 1 piece honeydew melon (5 oz) • 1/2 banana • Juice from 4 oranges • 2 tbs wheat germ • Pinch of ground ginger

Peel the melon, remove the seeds, and cut into small cubes. Peel and slice the banana. Using a hand blender or regular blender, puree the fruit along with the orange juice, wheat germ, and ground ginger. Pour into two large glasses and serve with large straws.

PER SERVING: 155 calories • 4 g protein • 1 g fat • 31 g carbohydrates

Creamy Citrus
enhances mental fitness
Cooler

Serves 2: 8 oz low-fat kefir or plain yogurt • 7 oz freshly squeezed orange juice • Juice from 1 lime • 2 tbs granulated lecithin (from the health-food store) • 1 tbs honey • 1/4 tsp vanilla powder

With a hand blender or regular blender, vigorously blend the kefir or yogurt, orange juice, and lime juice with the granulated lecithin and two thirds of the honey. Sweeten to taste with the remaining honey. Pour the mixture into two glasses and sprinkle with the vanilla powder.

PER SERVING: 280 calories • 5 g protein • 17 g fat • 23 g carbohydrates

Tangy Tomato-
best served chilled
Basil Shake

Serves 2: 4 ripe tomatoes • 1/2 cup buttermilk • 1 tbs roughly chopped fresh basil • Pinch of sugar • Tabasco sauce to taste

Briefly plunge the tomatoes into boiling water and remove the skins. Remove the stems, and cut the tomato into small pieces. With a hand blender or regular blender, thoroughly puree the tomatoes, the buttermilk, the basil, and the sugar. Season with Tabasco, adding only one drop at a time. Pour the drink into two glasses and serve.

PER SERVING: 77 calories • 4 g protein • 1 g fat • 14 g carbohydrates

Vegetable Curry
spiced with red chiles and fresh ginger
with Peanuts

Cook the rice in the water, according to the directions on the package. Peel the ginger, garlic, and shallots and cut them into fine dice. Slit open the chiles, then trim, wash, and cut into thin rings.

Wash and trim the broccoli and separate into small florets. Wash and peel the carrots and slice them diagonally. Cut the bell pepper in half, remove the stem, seeds, and ribs, then wash and cut into strips. Clean and trim the mushrooms and cut into quarters. Heat the oil in a wok or large skillet over high heat. Briefly stir-fry the ginger, garlic, shallots, and chiles. Stir in the curry paste and briefly stir-fry. Gradually add the coconut milk, then stir in the broccoli and carrots and stir-fry about 3 more minutes. Add the remaining vegetables and continue to cook until everything is tender-crisp. Season to taste with salt and lemon juice. Coarsely chop the peanuts, then sprinkle over the curry along with the cilantro leaves. Arrange on plates with the rice and serve.

Serves 2:

1/2 cup basmati rice

1 cup water

1-inch piece fresh ginger

1 clove garlic

2 shallots

1–2 red chiles

8 oz broccoli

2 carrots

1 yellow bell pepper

4 oz mushrooms

1 tbs vegetable oil

2 tsp red curry paste

1 1/4 cups unsweetened coconut milk

Salt to taste

1–2 tsp fresh lemon juice

2 tbs salted peanuts

2 tbs chopped fresh cilantro

PER SERVING: 385 calories • 14 g protein • 12 g fat • 60 g carbohydrates

Corn Fritters

particularly tasty with a green salad

with Shrimp

Drain the corn in a sieve, then, using a hand blender or regular blender, coarsely puree it with 1 heaping tbs of the cottage cheese. Pour the remaining cottage cheese into a cheesecloth-lined sieve and let drain.

Rinse the shrimp, pat dry, and coarsely chop. Wash, peel, and finely grate the carrot. In a bowl, mix the shrimp and grated carrot with the corn. Peel and mince the garlic and add to the bowl. Stir in the egg yolk, grated coconut, salt, pepper, and cornmeal or flour until the batter is uniform. Heat the oil in a skillet over medium-high heat. From the batter, spoon out six fritters into the pan and fry until golden brown on both sides, about 3 minutes per side. Once cooked, place the fritters on paper towels to absorb excess oil.

Serves 2:
4 oz canned corn kernels
1/2 cup cottage cheese
2 oz shrimp, peeled
1 small carrot
1 small clove garlic
1 egg yolk
2 tbs grated unsweetened coconut
Salt to taste
Black pepper to taste
1 tbs cornmeal or flour
2–3 tbs vegetable oil
1 tbs minced fresh Italian parsley

Mix the drained cottage cheese with the parsley. Arrange the fritters on plates, adding a dollop of the cottage cheese mixture to the middle of each fritter, and serve warm.

PER SERVING: 300 calories • 13 g protein • 21 g fat • 16 g carbohydrates

Spaghetti with Broccoli

studded with prosciutto and capers

Cream Sauce

Coarsely chop 1 tbs of the pistachios, then finely chop the rest. Drain the capers well. Wash and trim the broccoli, then separate into florets and blanch in boiling salted water for 3 minutes. Drain the broccoli, immediately plunge into ice-cold water, then drain well in a sieve.

Bring a generous amount of salted water to a boil and cook the spaghetti according to the directions on the package until slightly firm to the bite, al dente. Meanwhile, peel and mince the shallot. Heat the oil in a saucepan over medium heat, add the shallot and sauté briefly. Add half the broccoli, the vegetable stock, the yogurt, and the finely chopped pistachios. With a hand blender or regular blender, puree everything to create a creamy sauce. Season with salt, pepper, and lemon juice. Cut the prosciutto into wide strips. Warm the remaining broccoli florets in the sauce. Drain the spaghetti, then serve in bowls with the broccoli cream sauce and the strips of prosciutto. Garnish with the capers and the coarsely chopped pistachios.

Serves 2:

2 tbs shelled pistachios

1-2 tbs small capers

10 oz broccoli

Salt to taste

8 oz spaghetti

1 shallot

1 tbs vegetable oil

2/3 cup vegetable stock

1/2 cup plain yogurt

Black pepper to taste

2 tsp fresh lemon juice

2 oz prosciutto, thinly sliced

PER SERVING: 590 calories • 28 g protein • 17 g fat • 83 g carbohydrates

Tex-Mex Wrap

supplies a burst of energy

with Avocado

Wash the tomato, remove the stem, and dice. Trim and wash the bell pepper, then cut into fine dice. Wash and trim the celery, then cut into fine dice. Peel the avocado, cut

Serves 2:

1 tomato
1/2 yellow bell pepper
1/2 stalk celery
1 small ripe avocado
1–2 tbs fresh lemon juice
1 tbs plain yogurt
2 tbs minced fresh cilantro or Italian parsley
Salt to taste
Hot pepper sauce to taste
2 flour tortillas (about 6 inches in diameter)

in half lengthwise and remove the pit. Finely dice one half of the avocado, then mash the other half with 1 tbs lemon juice, and the yogurt. Gently mix the mashed avocado with the diced avocado, the diced vegetables, and 1 1/2 tbs of the minced cilantro or parsley. Season to taste with salt, hot sauce, and the remaining lemon juice.

Spoon the filling onto the two tortillas, roll them up, then cover and refrigerate until ready to serve. When you are ready, cut the Tex-Mex wraps in half at a diagonal and arrange on plates. Garnish with the remaining cilantro or parsley leaves.

Versatile wraps

You can serve these Tex-Mex wraps alone or with a large green salad, or serve them as an unusual side dish next to fast-cooking meat, such as chicken, fish, or steak.

PER SERVING:

220 calories

7 g protein

9 g fat

29 g carbohydrates

Vegetable Stew

provides serotonin and iron for more vitality

with Millet

Bring the millet and 2/3 cup of the vegetable stock to a boil, cover, turn off the heat, and let the millet stand for about 20 minutes. Wash and peel the carrots and kohlrabi. Slice the carrots and dice the kohlrabi. Peel the onion and cut into fine dice.

Serves 2:
1/3 cup millet
4 cups vegetable stock
8 oz carrots
1 bulb kohlrabi
1 onion
2 tbs olive oil
1–2 tsp hot mustard
1 bay leaf
Salt to taste
Pepper to taste
Handful of fresh spinach leaves
2 tomatoes
5 oz frozen peas
1 clove garlic
3 tbs chopped fresh Italian parsley or chives

Heat the oil in a saucepan over medium heat. Briefly sauté the carrots, kohlrabi, and onion in the oil, then add the remaining 3 1/3 cups vegetable stock, mustard, bay leaf, and a little salt and pepper. Bring to a boil, cover, reduce the heat to low, and simmer for 10 minutes.

Wash and sort the spinach, remove any large stems, then tear the leaves into pieces. Wash and dice the tomatoes, removing the stems. Add the spinach, tomatoes, and peas to the pot and simmer another 10 minutes. Peel and mince the garlic, and add to the vegetables. Stir in the parsley or chives and the millet, season to taste with salt and pepper, and serve immediately.

Millet

This small, yellow grain is packed with important nutrients. Millet is a rich source of iron, manganese, copper, magnesium, fluorine, silicic acid, B-vitamins, and lecithin, which makes it a great brain food. This powerhouse grain enhances alertness, vitality, and your overall mood.

PER SERVING:

430 calories

12 g protein

15 g fat

60 g carbohydrates

Zucchini Pancakes
quickly restores lost energy
with Cured Salmon

In a bowl, combine the eggs, flour, pinch of salt, and thyme and stir into a thick batter using a wire whisk. Cover the bowl and refrigerate for 15 minutes. Peel the shallot and cut into very fine dice. Wash and trim the zucchini, then coarsely grate it using a vegetable grater. Stir the shallot and grated zucchini into the batter along with the heavy cream, then season with salt and pepper.

In a large skillet, heat the oil over medium heat. From the batter, spoon about 6-8 portions of the batter into the hot oil and fry until golden brown (about 3 minutes per side), then set aside onto paper towels to absorb any excess oil.

Cut the salmon into wide strips and arrange on plates with the zucchini pancakes. Stir together the yogurt and lime juice and drizzle over the salmon strips.

Serves 2:

2 eggs

1/3 cup flour

Salt to taste

1 tsp dried thyme

1 shallot

8 oz zucchini

2 tbs heavy cream

Black pepper to taste

2–3 tbs vegetable oil

2 oz cured salmon (such as gravlax)

3 tbs low-fat plain yogurt

2-3 tsp fresh lime juice

PER SERVING: 420 calories • 18 g protein • 24 g fat • 33 g carbohydrates

Green Vegetables with Tuna Sauce

full of relaxing calcium and magnesium

Wash and trim the vegetables. Peel the lower third of the asparagus stalks. Cut the zucchini in quarters lengthwise, and cut the celery in half lengthwise. Cut the asparagus, zucchini, celery, and green onions into pieces roughly the size of the green beans.

Wash the lime in hot water, pat dry, then grate the zest and squeeze the juice. Add the vegetables to a shallow bowl, lightly salt and pepper, and sprinkle with the lime zest. Wash the parsley and set aside three sprigs.

Pour the water into a wide saucepan, then add 1/2 tsp salt, and the asparagus. Place a steamer rack on top of the asparagus and set the shallow bowl on a steam rack. Cover the pot and steam the vegetables for 10-12 minutes, until tender-crisp.

Drain the tuna, then finely puree with the crème fraîche and 2 tbs lime juice. Mince the parsley and stir it into the sauce along with the capers. Season the sauce to taste and serve with the vegetables.

Serves 2:

28 oz mixed green vegetables (such as asparagus, zucchini, celery, green beans, green onions, snow peas)

1 lime

Salt to taste

White pepper to taste

3 sprigs fresh Italian parsley

3/4 cup water

1 small can water-packed tuna (3 oz)

1 tbs crème fraîche

2 tsp small capers

Green vegetables for more vitality

Some say that green is the color of hope. If you're feeling run-down, you should treat yourself to green vegetables, whether raw or carefully cooked to preserve their invigorating vitamins and nutrients. Green vegetables calm, relax, and reduce aggression.

PER SERVING:

235 calories

24 g protein

14 g fat

30 g carbohydrates

Stuffed

with spicy almond-spiked spinach

Potatoes

Thoroughly wash the potatoes under running water using a brush, then boil unpeeled for 30 minutes. Wash and sort the spinach, and remove any large stems. Add the wet spinach to a skillet and wilt over high heat. Transfer the spinach to a sieve, press out most of the liquid, then chop coarsely. Wash the zucchini half and grate coarsely. Peel and dice the onion. Preheat the oven to 425°F. Heat the oil in a skillet over medium heat. Add the onion and grated zucchini and sauté for 2 minutes. Drain the potatoes, then cut in half lengthwise and scoop out some of the flesh to create a cavity, saving the scooped-out potato in a bowl.

Mash the scooped-out potato with the spinach, the onion-zucchini mixture, the egg, Gorgonzola cheese, almonds, and yogurt. Season the filling with salt and pepper. Fill the potato shells with the spinach mixture, dividing evenly. Arrange the filled potatoes on a baking sheet and bake in the middle of the oven for about 15 minutes, until hot.

Serves 2:
3 large boiling potatoes (about 7–9 oz each)
8 oz fresh spinach
1/2 zucchini
1 onion
2 tbs olive oil
1 egg
About 2 oz Gorgonzola cheese
1/4 cup almonds, very finely chopped
2-3 tbs plain whole-milk yogurt
Salt to taste
Pepper to taste

Potatoes

Along with vitamins, minerals, and fiber, potatoes also contain phenylalanine, an amino acid that is a precursor to norepinepherine, one of the most important happiness hormones. Norepinepherine refreshes and motivates, strengthens nerves and provides a feeling of well-being.

PER SERVING:

645 calories

24 g protein

34 g fat

62 g carbohydrates

Potatoes with Tomato-

with invigorating exotic spices

Yogurt Sauce

Mix the spices together. To prepare the sauce, wash and halve the tomatoes, remove the stems and seeds, and cut into a small dice. Mix the yogurt with the diced tomatoes and one quarter of the spice mixture. Wash the cilantro or parsley, shake dry, remove the leaves from the stems, and mince the leaves. Mix half of the minced cilantro or parsley into the tomato-yogurt mixture. Season the sauce with salt and pepper, cover, and refrigerate.

Thoroughly wash the potatoes under running water using a brush, then dry and cut the unpeeled potatoes into quarters. Peel the shallots and cut into quarters lengthwise. Heat the oil in a large skillet over medium heat. Add the potatoes and shallots and sprinkle with the remaining spice mixture.

Sauté the potatoes and shallots for about 10 minutes, stirring frequently, then reduce the heat and sauté for about 20 more minutes until tender, turning occasionally. Season the potatoes to taste with salt and pepper. Garnish with the remaining cilantro or parsley and serve with the tomato-yogurt sauce.

Serves 2:

1 tsp ground coriander

1 tsp ground cumin

1/4 tsp ground cardamom

2 dashes ground ginger

Dash each of: ground allspice, cinnamon, and turmeric

Dash of ground nutmeg

2 tomatoes

3/4 cup plain whole-milk yogurt

5 sprigs fresh cilantro or Italian parsley

Salt to taste

Pepper to taste

Generous 1 lb firm potatoes

4 shallots

1 tbs vegetable oil

PER SERVING: 280 calories • 8 g protein • 11 g fat • 38 g carbohydrates

Halibut with a Rice

high in easily digestible protein and fiber

and Vegetable Crust

Cook the rice in the water, according to the directions on the package.

Preheat the oven to 400° F. Wash the halibut fillets in cold water, pat dry, season with salt and pepper, and drizzle with the lemon juice. Oil a flat ovenproof pan.

Wash the leek and the carrot. Trim the leek, peel the carrot, and cut both into very thin strips or into cubes. Heat the butter in a skillet over medium heat until it bubbles, then add the vegetables and sauté for 2 minutes. Season with salt and pepper. Drain the rice if necessary. Gently stir the rice, parsley, and cheese into the vegetable mixture.

Arrange the halibut fillets next to each other in the ovenproof pan. Spread the rice and vegetable mixture over the halibut, dividing evenly and patting down slightly. Bake the fish in the middle of the oven for 20–25 minutes until a light crust has formed and the fish is cooked through. Garnish with the lemon slices, watercress and herbs and serve.

Serves 2:

1/4 cup brown rice

2 halibut fillets (about 4 oz each)

1/2 cup water

Salt to taste

White pepper to taste

1 tbs fresh lemon juice

Oil for the pan

1/2 leek

1 carrot

1/2 tbs butter

1 tbs minced fresh Italian parsley

2 tbs grated Swiss cheese

4 thin lemon slices

Watercress or parsley leaves

PER SERVING: 520 calories • 10 g protein • 14 g fat • 50 g carbohydrates

Herbed Mackerel

with valuable fatty acids and nutrients

in Foil

Preheat the oven to 350°F. Rinse the mackerels and pat dry. Season all sides with salt, pepper, and lemon juice and sprinkle with 3 tbs of the dill.

Serves 2:
2 mackerel fillets
Salt to taste
White pepper to taste
2 tsp fresh lemon juice
6 tbs minced fresh dill
3/4 cup sour cream
1/4 cup milk
2 tbs cream-style horseradish
1 tbs capers
1–2 tsp sweet mustard

Place the fillets next to each other on two large sheets of aluminum foil (shiny side up). Fold the foil around the fish to make a tightly sealed package. Prick a hole in the top for a steam vent. Place on an unheated rack and bake the fish in the middle of the oven for 20 minutes.

Beat the sour cream with the milk and the horseradish until creamy. Finely chop the capers and fold into the mixture. Season the mixture to taste with mustard, salt, and pepper. Gently stir in the remaining 3 tbs dill. Serve the horseradish-caper cream with the herbed mackerel.

Mackerel

Mackerel is a true fitness fish. Its high content of potassium, iodine, nerve-strengthening niacin, vitamins D, B6, B12, valuable amino acids, and omega-3 fatty acids all provide for a turbo effect that lightens your mood and gives you power.

PER SERVING:

437 calories

42 g protein

26 g fat

8 g carbohydrates

Baked Tuna
nutrients that invigorate the senses
with Fennel

Rinse the tuna, pat dry, and place on a plate. Drizzle the tuna with lemon juice and 1 tbs of the anise liqueur, then refrigerate. Preheat the oven to 425°F. Wash and trim the fennel bulbs, cut in half, and then cut into thin slices. Set aside the fennel fronds.

Peel the shallot and finely chop. Oil an ovenproof pan. Arrange the fennel, shallot, and oregano in the pan, then season with salt and pepper and drizzle with 2 tsp oil. Pour in the vegetable stock and the remaining anise liqueur.

Bake the fennel in the middle of the oven for 15 minutes, stirring the fennel once halfway through. Wash the tomatoes, remove the stems, and dice. Season the fish with salt and pepper, then arrange on top of the fennel. Spread the diced tomatoes over the fish, and arrange dabs of butter on top. Bake for about another 15 minutes, until the fish is cooked through. Chop the fennel fronds and sprinkle over the fish.

Serves 2:
2 fresh tuna fillets (about 4 oz each)
1 tbs fresh lemon juice
1/4 cup anise liqueur (such as Pernod or ouzo)
12 oz small fennel bulbs
1 shallot
Oil for the pan
2 sprigs fresh oregano
2 tsp olive oil
Salt to taste
Black pepper to taste
2/3 cup vegetable stock
3 tomatoes
1 tbs butter

Fennel

Fennel has a beneficial effect on the mind and body. Calcium, one of its nutrients, plays an important role for nerves and the brain. Iron is essential for a good oxygen supply and fennel's ethereal oils calm and relax the mind.

PER SERVING:

690 calories

49 g protein

40 g fat

20 g carbohydrates

Curried Fish

exotic, hearty, & truly satisfying

Soup

Serves 2:
1 small zucchini
2 small red bell peppers
2 tbs vegetable oil
9 oz firm potatoes
1 shallot
1 clove garlic
2 tbs grated unsweetened coconut
1–2 tsp curry powder
2 cups vegetable stock
1 2/3 cups fish stock or clam juice
Salt to taste
8 oz perch or other mild white fish fillets
4 large shrimp, peeled and deveined
Fresh dill leaves

Wash and trim the zucchini, then cut into small dice. Cut the bell peppers in half, then remove the stems, seeds, and ribs. Wash the halves and cut into small dice. Heat 1 tbs of the oil in a saucepan over medium heat, add the diced vegetables, and sauté for 1 minute. Afterward, transfer the vegetables to a plate, cover, and set aside. Wash, peel, and dice the potatoes. Peel the shallot and garlic, and cut both into fine dice.

Heat the remaining 1 tbs oil in the saucepan over medium heat, add the potatoes, shallot, and garlic and sauté briefly. Stir in the grated coconut and curry powder and sauté lightly with the vegetables. Pour in the vegetable stock, cover, and simmer for 10 minutes over low heat. Add the reserved vegetables, the fish stock, and a little salt, cover, and simmer for 5 minutes over low heat. Rinse and pat dry the fish and shrimp. Cut the fish into pieces (not too small). Remove about 1/4 of the vegetables from the stock and puree in a blender or food processor. Add the puree back to the soup along with the fish and shrimp. Cover and cook over low heat for about 4 minutes, or until the fish is just cooked through. Season the soup to taste, garnish with dill leaves, and serve.

PER SERVING: 390 calories • 31 g protein • 17 g fat • 27 g carbohydrates

Lamb Kebabs with

rich in protein and carbohydrates

Sesame Rice

Score the tops of the tomatoes, then blanch for several seconds in boiling water. Lift out the tomatoes, remove the skins, stems, and seeds, then cut the tomato flesh into small pieces. Peel the

Serves 2:

18 oz ripe tomatoes
1 clove garlic
1 small onion
1 1/2 tbs olive oil
Salt to taste
Black pepper to taste
1 tsp maple syrup
3/4 cup long-grain rice
1 1/2 cups water
10 oz lamb shoulder
1 yellow bell pepper
2 tbs sesame seeds
1 tbs capers

garlic and onion, then cut into fine dice. Heat 2 tsp of the oil in skillet over medium heat and sauté the garlic and onion until translucent. Add the tomatoes, salt, pepper, and maple syrup, then cover and simmer gently for 20 minutes. Cook the rice in the water, according to the directions on the package. Cut the meat into bite-sized cubes. Cut the bell pepper in half, remove the stem, seeds, and ribs, then wash and cut into pieces slightly larger than the meat cubes. Thread the meat and bell pepper onto the soaked skewers, alternating between the two.

Heat the broiler. Place the kebabs on a broiling pan and broil about 4 inches from the heat source for about 4 to 6 minutes, turning once, for medium-rare meat. Season the kebabs with salt and pepper. Toast the sesame seeds in a dry nonstick skillet and mix into the rice. Stir the capers into the tomato sauce and season to taste. Serve the kebabs on the rice and accompany with the sauce.

Sesame seeds

Sesame seeds promote fitness and keep you young. Nutrients include calcium, selenium, silicic acid, and lecithin.

PER SERVING:

585 calories

41 g protein

15 g fat

71 g carbohydrates

Honey-Marinated
with zucchini and sun-dried tomatoes
Rump Steaks

Stir together the olive oil, thyme, honey, and a pinch of pepper. Peel and mince the garlic, and add it to the honey mixture. Pat dry the rump steaks, brush all sides with the marinade, cover and marinate in the refrigerator for 2 hours.

Drain the tomatoes in a sieve, taking care to save the oil. Wash and trim the zucchini, cut in half lengthwise, then slice. Cut the tomatoes into strips. Remove the steaks from the marinade and let drain. In a nonstick skillet over medium-high heat quickly sear the steaks for 2 minutes on each side. Salt the steaks, remove from the pan, cover and keep warm. Slowly add the remaining marinade to the pan.

Add the zucchini slices, tomato strips, and the oil from the tomatoes to the pan and sauté for 3 minutes, stirring constantly. Season the vegetables with salt, pepper, sugar, and vinegar. Serve the vegetables with the steaks.

Serves 2:

2 tbs olive oil
1/2 tsp dried thyme
2 tsp floral honey
Black pepper to taste
1 clove garlic
2 rump steaks (about 5 oz each)
2 oz oil-packed sun-dried tomatoes
10 oz zucchini
Salt to taste
Pinch of sugar
1–2 tbs balsamic vinegar

PER SERVING: 585 calories • 41 g protein • 15 g fat • 71 g carbohydrates

Spicy Chicken with
a light and fruity dish from South America
Fresh Mango Sauce

Peel the mango and cut away the fruit from the large flat seed in wide strips. Cut the mango strips into pieces and drizzle with lemon juice. For the sauce, finely puree one third of the mango pieces with the yogurt in a blender or food processor. Wash the lettuce leaves, shake dry, and tear into large pieces. Slit open the chile, trim, and cut into thin rings. Rinse and pat dry the chicken and cut into finger-width strips. Heat the oil in a nonstick skillet over medium-high heat, add the chicken strips and chile and sauté on all sides for about 4 minutes until golden brown and cooked through. Season with salt. Arrange the chicken and chile, the lettuce, and the mango pieces on plates and drizzle with the mango sauce. Serve with tortilla chips.

Serves 2:

1 ripe mango

2 tbs fresh lemon juice

2 oz plain whole-milk yogurt

4 leaves leaf lettuce

1 red chile

10 oz boneless, skinless chicken breast

2 tbs vegetable oil

Salt to taste

About 2 oz tortilla chips

Chicken

Chicken is low in fat and easy to digest, and it is also an excellent source of vitamins, minerals, and valuable amino acids, which are necessary for generating neurotransmitters. This combination supplies energy and motivation, and also enhances your sense of well-being.

PER SERVING:

395 calories

32 g protein

17 g fat

27 g carbohydrates

Chocolate
with cardamom and coffee liqueur
Mousse

Break 3 oz of the chocolate into pieces and melt in a bowl placed in a warm water bath, then let cool until lukewarm. Dissolve the espresso in the hot water, then stir in the coffee liqueur and cardamom.

Separate the egg. In separate bowls, beat the egg white and the heavy cream until stiff. Combine the egg yolk, vanilla extract, confectioners' sugar, and lukewarm water and beat until creamy and the sugar is completely dissolved. Gradually stir in the espresso-cardamom mixture, then the lukewarm chocolate. Then fold in the whipped cream, and finally the egg white. Spoon the mousse into two dessert glasses, cover, and refrigerate for at least 2 hours or overnight. Using a vegetable peeler, shave the remaining chocolate and sprinkle over the mousse. Serve with the strawberries, if desired.

Serves 2:

4 oz bittersweet chocolate

2 tsp instant espresso

2 tbs hot water

2 tbs coffee liqueur

1/2 tsp ground cardamom

1 egg

1/3 cup heavy cream

1/2 tsp vanilla extract

1 tbs confectioners' sugar

1 tbs lukewarm water

Sliced fresh strawberries

Choosing chocolate

It can't be denied that chocolate helps with life's frustrations, but ideally you should choose as dark a chocolate as possible; the higher the percentage of cocoa and the lower the percentage of sugar, the better off you'll be. In the end, it isn't the quantity you consume that is important, but rather that you enjoy chocolate dishes slowly and consciously.

PER SERVING:

455 calories

7 g protein

30 g fat

39 g carbohydrates

Mascarpone-
with Italian almond cookies
Cherry Trifles

Serves 2:

2 tbs sliced almonds

8 oz mascarpone cheese

Pinch of vanilla powder

2 tbs sugar

1/4 cup milk

8 oz sweet cherries

About 2 oz amarettini (small Italian almond cookies)

2 tbs cream sherry

Toast the sliced almonds in a small nonstick skillet until golden brown, stirring constantly. Immediately remove from the heat and set aside to cool. Using a wire whisk, beat the mascarpone cheese, vanilla, sugar, and milk in a bowl until creamy, then cover and refrigerate.

Wash the cherries, dry carefully, then remove the stems and pits. Using a knife, lightly crush the cookies into large pieces, then drizzle with the sherry. Spoon loose layers of the mascarpone cream, the crushed cookies, and the cherries into two tall glasses. Garnish with the sliced almonds.

Cherries

Sweet cherries are the best type of cherries for eating. They contain more minerals and trace elements than sour cherries. The darker the color of a fruit, the riper and more aromatic it is.

PER SERVING:

735 calories

9 g protein

59 g fat

37 g carbohydrates

Yogurt-Berry
refreshing and invigorating
Parfait

In a saucepan, bring a few inches of water to a boil. In a heatproof mixing bowl, whip the egg yolks, honey, sugar, and ginger until creamy. Place the bowl in the hot water bath (no longer boiling) and briskly whip the batter with a wire whisk until it forms a thick froth. Remove from the hot water bath and continue to beat while the batter cools.

In another bowl, whip the cream until stiff. First fold the whipped cream into the egg yolk mixture, then fold in the yogurt. Spoon the mixture into 2 bowls or parfait glasses, cover, and place in the freezer for at least 3 hours.

About 20 minutes before serving, remove the parfait from the freezer. Sort and wash the berries and pat dry. Garnish the parfait with berries and dust with confectioners' sugar.

Serves 2:

2 egg yolks

3 tsp honey

1 tbs sugar

2 pinches ground ginger

1/3 cup heavy cream

2 oz low-fat plain yogurt

9 oz strawberries or raspberries

Confectioners' sugar

Honey

Honey is effective on many levels. Its chromium promotes the utilization of glucose in the brain, which also supplies energy. Acetylcholine accelerates the transmission of signals between nerve cells, and the smooth consistency of honey releases soothing reflexes in the nervous system.

PER SERVING:

335 calories

7 g protein

19 g fat

35 g carbohydrates

Figs with Frothy
with a relaxing fragrance
Cinnamon Sauce

Serves 2:

1 small orange

3 ripe figs

1 egg yolk

1 tbs confectioners' sugar

2 pinches ground cinnamon

1/2 cup milk

With a long sharp knife, carefully remove the peel from the orange, taking care to remove the white pith. Cut between the fruit's membranes to remove the orange "fillets;" make sure to remove the seeds and collect the juice that escapes. Place 3 sections of orange in a sieve and mash with a spoon, catching the resulting juice and mixing it with the other juice (you should have about 1/4 cup of juice). Carefully wash the figs, pat dry, and slice. Place the fig slices in a bowl, drizzle with 2 tbs of the orange juice, cover, and set aside.

In a saucepan, bring a few inches of water to a boil. In a heatproof mixing bowl, whisk the egg yolk with the confectioners' sugar, cinnamon, and the remaining 2 tbs orange juice until creamy. Place the bowl over the hot water bath (no longer boiling) and add the milk. Vigorously beat the mixture with a wire whisk until a frothy sauce is formed.

Arrange the figs, remaining orange fillets, and the cinnamon sauce in bowls and serve immediately.

Figs
Make sure to buy truly ripe figs. Only figs that are ripe have that unmistakable aroma and fragrance. This fruit tastes best when chilled. If you don't wish to eat the skin, you can also carefully peel the figs.

PER SERVING:

135 calories

4 g protein

5 g fat

17 g carbohydrates

Pineapple-
with lime juice and sesame brittle
Papaya Salad

Serves 2: 2 tbs sesame seeds • 2 tbs sugar • 1 tsp vegetable oil • 1/4 fresh pineapple • 1 kiwi • 1 small ripe papaya • 2 tbs fresh lime juice • Pinch of vanilla powder

In a dry nonstick skillet, brown the sesame seeds and sugar, stirring constantly. Pour the mixture onto an oiled sheet of aluminum foil and let cool. Peel the pineapple, cut in half lengthwise, and cut into pieces. Peel the kiwi and papaya. Cut the papaya in half lengthwise and remove the seeds. Slice the kiwi and papaya. Stir together the lime juice and vanilla, then coat the fruit in the juice. Crumble the sesame brittle and sprinkle over the salad.

PER SERVING: 165 calories • 2 g protein • 5 g fat • 39 g carbohydrates

Dates with
tastes best when chilled
Minted Yogurt

Serves 2: 8 oz low-fat plain yogurt • 2 sprigs fresh mint • 2 tbs sugar • 1/2 tsp vanilla extract • 1 tbs chopped hazelnuts • 2 tbs fresh lemon juice • 8 fresh dates

Pour the yogurt into a cheesecloth-lined sieve, suspend the sieve over a bowl, and let it drain for 30 minutes in the refrigerator. Transfer the yogurt to a bowl. Wash the mint and dry, remove the leaves from the stems and chop coarsely. Place the mint, sugar, vanilla, and nuts in a food processor and process until fine. Stir the mint mixture into the yogurt and add lemon juice. Wash and dry the dates, remove the pits and cut lengthwise into pieces. Serve dates with the minted yogurt for dipping.

PER SERVING: 249 calories • 7 g protein • 5 g fat • 48 g carbohydrates

Apricot-Cream
garnished with pistachios
Cheese Gratin

Preheat oven to 425°F. Wash the apricots, dry well, then cut in half and remove the pits. Cut the fruit into thick wedges and drizzle with the apricot liqueur.

Separate the egg. Beat the egg white until stiff. Mix the cream cheese with the sugar, vanilla, and egg yolk until smooth. Fold the egg white into the cream cheese mixture. Lightly butter 2 small gratin dishes, then pour the cream cheese mixture into the pans and fan out the apricot wedges on top.

Bake the gratin in the middle of the oven for 10 minutes, then increase the oven heat to 475°F. Bake for an additional 5 minutes until the surface of the gratin is golden brown. Garnish with pistachios and serve warm.

Serves 2:

8 oz fresh apricots

1 tbs apricot liqueur

1 egg

2 tbs confectioners' sugar

1/2 tsp vanilla extract

4 oz cream cheese, softened

1/2 tsp soft butter

1 tbs chopped pistachios

Easy to adapt

Depending on the season and your appetite, you can easily substitute other fruits in this dessert. Other tasty choices include bananas, figs, pineapple, oranges, berries, and cherries. You can also use a mixture of fruits.

PER SERVING:

365 calories

9 g protein

25 g fat

24 g carbohydrates

Index

Abbreviations

tsp = teaspoon
tbs = tablespoon

Published originally under the title
REZEPTE FUER GUTE LAUNE,
©1999 Gräfe und Unzer Verlag GmbH,
Munich
English translation for the U.S. edition:
©2001 Silverback Books, Inc.

Project editor: Lisa M. Tooker
Editors: Ina Schröter, Jennifer Newens, CCP
Readers: Maryna Zimdars,
Vené Franco
Translator: Heather Bock
Layout: Heinz Kraxenberger
Production: Helmut Giersberg,
Shanti Nelson
Photos: FoodPhotography Eising
Typesetting: Johannes Kojer
Reproduction: Repro Schmidt, Dornbirn
Printing: Appl, Wemding
Binding: Sellier, Freising

Printed in Hong Kong through Global
Interprint, Santa Rosa, California

ISBN: 1-930603-85-1

Caution

The techniques and recipes in this book are
to be used at the reader's sole discretion and
risk. Always consult a doctor before
beginning a new eating plan.

Marlisa Szwillus

After receiving a degree in Nutrition and
Home Economics, Szwillus became an editor
for a well-known magazine. For several years,
she managed the cooking department for one
of Europe's largest food magazines. Since
1993, she has been a freelance food journalist
and author in Munich. She is a member of
the German Food Editors Club and, in her
role as an expert, always attempts to link
healthy eating with culinary enjoyment.

Susie M. and Pete Eising

The Eising's have studios in Germany, and in
the United States. They studied at the Munich
Academy of Photography, where they
established their own studio for food
photography in 1991.

For this book:
Photographic layout:
Martina Görach
Food styling:
Monika Schuster

Our thanks for their support during
photo production:
Adornetto (Kirchheim)
Designers Guild (Germany)
LSA (London)
Mercantile (Planegg)
Perles d'Asie (Paris)

SILVERBACK

BOOKS, INC.